New Power

Acknowledgments: Several of these poems have previously appeared in *The Fiddlehead, Undertow, Afterthoughts, Centrepoint, The Sound* and the *We'moon Woman's Datebook.*

Author photo on back cover by Warren Rudd
Author photo on front cover by Jenson
Cover photo by Christine Lowther
Design and in-house editing by Joe Blades
Printed and bound in Canada by Sentinel Printing, Yarmouth NS.
Printed on Sandpiper Lily of the Valley vellum finish acid-free papers (100% non-bleached,non-deinked, post-consumer fibers).

The Publisher gratefully acknowledges the support of the Canada Council for the Arts and the New Brunswick Department of Economic Development, Tourism and Culture.

THE CANADA COUNCIL | LE CONSEIL DES ARTS
FOR THE ARTS | DU CANADA

Canadian Cataloguing in Publication Data
Lowther, Christine, 1967-

    New power

    Poems.
    ISBN 0-921411-94-4

I. Title.

PS8597.O898N49 1999   C811'.54   C99-950088-0
PR9199.3.L68N49 1999

Broken Jaw Press
Box 596 Stn A   tel / fax 506 454-5127
Fredericton NB E3B 5A6   www.brokenjaw.com
Canada   jblades@nbnet.nb.ca

New Power

Christine Lowther

Fredericton • Canada

Acknowledgements

First I hail the Clayoquot Writers' Group: Sherry Merk, Betty Krawczyk, Ellen Tolsen, Shirley Langer, Nicole Gervais, Gisele Martin, Jan Bate, Janice Lore, Karen Lloyd, Joanna Streetly, Kathy Shaw and Mary-Ann Mikolic. Mary Hilbert first insisted I send my poems "out, tout de suite". Joy Kogawa said the magic words (and did so much more!). Fred Cogswell knew where to send them; Joe Blades offerred to give them back. My gratitude to Susan Musgrave, Penn Kemp, Lorraine Vernon, Christine Wiesenthal, Kathy Lyons, Beth Lowther, Cathy Ford, Keith Harrison, George Walkem and Toby Brooks for support and advice. Sushil Saini and Helen Rudd, cheers very much for being there. I appreciate the times I was able to expose some of these poems at readings, so thank you Wildside Readers and Writers of Tofino, League organizers of the Pat Lowther Award Benefit in May 98, and *A Sad and Beautiful World* on CFUV. Perhaps the process all started with the Pat Lowther 20-year memorial reading in Toronto in 95. That was Toby, and Della Golland — and cheers to everyone who took part in that. Beth Goobie believed in me. Deep thanks to so many people who reviewed *Time Capsule*, while I'm at it. Thanks to Guy Chadsey, Yvonne Hunter and the Literary Press Group of Canada. Thanks also to Greg Gatenby and the Harbourfront Reading Series. And lastly, from the bottom of my heart I salute my partner, Warren Rudd.

This book is for the kids

At the age of seven, I lost both parents when my father murdered my mother. Both wrote poetry.

— C.L.

"Overcome any bitterness that may have come because you were not up to the magnitude of the pain that was entrusted to you. Like the Mother of the world, who carries the pain of the world in her heart, each one of us is part of her heart, and therefore endowed with a certain measure of cosmic pain. You are sharing in the totality of that pain. You are called upon to meet it in joy instead of self-pity."

Sufi saying quoted in *Coming Back to Life*
Joanna Macy and Molly Young Brown

"If we don't get swept away by our outrage, then we will see the cause of suffering more clearly."
— Pema Chödrön
When Things Fall Apart

PART ONE

Legacy

Historically the name of barons and lords,
corrupt politicians, cruel landowners
who evicted the orphanage
where Dorothy and Will Wordsworth
lived as children.
A name that evokes hatred
in the eyes of an old miner somewhere
north of England.

The name a woman was ironically known for
— the Poet, beloved;
the name a man died with
in obscurity, still complaining
of the lack of recognition
of his own writing.
Did she steal your name
and make it holy?
Are the women reclaiming it?
Would you roll over in your forgotten grave?

My name.

A Pagan's Comfort

The blood of the Goddess
birthed me.
My mother, at the top of the stairs,
sat down to rest
and the waterfall broke,
splashing down to my sister,
waiting on the landing below
young wide-eyed witness to nature's fast flow.

The blood of the Goddess
birthed me.
But first I wanted to test the air.
So I poked forth my hand
an expectant fist, fingers unfolding, coming unstuck
one from another in their dew, thumb
prying itself from my sticky palm;
the nurse held a mirror, and my mother
believed she had sprouted a new flower.

The blood of the Goddess
birthed me.
I emerged, seeing red.
I had known violence since conception,
sailing across the room inside her,
feeling the scarlet blow of impact
hearing his shouts through layers of cells.
My first sight was my mother's blood,
my nourisher, her pain, our connection of love.

The blood of the Goddess
birthed me
and all my tragic family
I was born with the blood on the wall
from my father's self-tormented head

I was born with the blood on the wall
from the death-knocks of his hammer on her skull
I am born, and I die, from the blood
of wretched Earth and countless women
on the hands of their men.

With every drop of Her blood spilt
we all endure a thousand deaths,
the very events which birth us again
kicking and screaming, covered in gore.
Let us always make an offering.

Memory

Age five or six. Helping to make placards. Two big old trees down the street are going to come down to make way for a housing development. Trying to print neatly on white cardboard with thick, smelly felt marker.

My sister, one year older, and I each take one of Mother's hands. We each hold a sign. I feel important as we join the neighbourhood picket, going round and round the block where the enormous giants stand on the edge of uncertainty. Days later she tries to break it to us gently that the trees are gone.

It must have been then that the seed of resistance was planted in my heart. Mum, would you be proud if you knew what a tree-hugger I am now?

Centre

in the centre of the house
the heavy wooden sliding doors are open.
here is an invisible line
between dining room and living room.
she stands, all three feet of her, indecisive
which room is safe?
her essence is fear.
she is sliced down the middle,
half for daddy, half for mama.
he wants more. she, tired of the struggle,
will settle for less.

in the centre the television music heralds
hockey night in canada   the beachcombers
the sunday singers   the roadrunner
m*a*s*h. the child hears
her mother exhale
a veil of cigarette smoke as she pours
over a book. drowns herself.
her body is seated at the dining table.
hollow, lost, a forced dissertion.
the candle's wick blown out
but better than dead.

the child can reach the scribbling table.
push a child-sized chair
out of the way.
here are piles of picture books
colouring books   crayons   felt markers
pencil crayons   she could almost eat
all the colours   "peach"
and "apricot" and "raspberry" are especially delicious.
here is a clean sheet of paper
waiting, begging for a sunset, a rainbow.

the lines of colour squiggle
over the table's rough surface
she wanted it to be perfect
amid the droning and smoking
and tense silence underneath it all.
she starts to cry   her mother does not look up
she cannot ask.

Mother

Every picture of you is a death mask.
pale, strange, distorted oval face
undefined brows over
big black eyes that *tell me nothing.*
there are no colour photographs.
your hair is always black,
thin and frizzy around the edges.
your mouth is unfamiliar,
full of crooked teeth.
your lips seem weathered,
bits breaking off under water

all of the edges begin to blur
from the water
even nipples, even black pubic hair
what was left of your head
must have sharpened the brains
of the fish who ate you
your eyes had flown
teeth knocked out when you were thrown onto wet stones
maybe your nose, solid, was still there
maybe your own hair clogged the nostrils
maybe you had swallowed your own hair
by the time you were discovered.

maybe your hands were wide open
like fins, or the wings of a river bird
everything people had known in your face
was found in your hands
every feather and scale a poem
but no one thought to look.
only police and corpse specialists
studied this poet's body,
not even your murderer-husband

was to be subjected to the sight of you.
he would have seen all of your poems
written in your palms,
along each finger and thumb
the grittier ones clamped down
under your nails

Would you look any different
in a colour photograph?
i see my sister and my aunt
in your wistful smile
but you exist in a vacant look of resignation —
a brutal life, a brutal death.

Your face seems scarred
made artistic by inner and outer suffering
"she was not photogenic"
"she was a beautiful woman"
if you were tormented,
thrown pregnant across the room over a chair
enough times would the shape
of your face flower with the pain
adding those experiences
to its waxy texture
Are you telling me this?

Twenty years after your death
the year i turned twenty-eight
i finally saw a silent film of you
on your wedding day,
eight days before you turned twenty-eight.
on my birthday i made an altar around your picture
grainy and grey, smiling over wedding flowers
i felt drawn by the colour blue
and placed blue beadwork, feathers, marbles, jewelry around you
then in the film i saw you were wearing turquoise

the next day i learned your eyes
were hazel like mine.

Moving Through

Five strikes to the head by my own hand.
My head.
I hit myself.

        hitting myself — a series of fast, hard blows
        to the side of the right temple
        nothing serious — no cutting of wrists
        no slashing of the face
        no burning of the arms
        no scalding of the palms of hands
nothing major enough for psychological intrigue
no call for help here
just hysteria, in the tradition of the female sex

Did i say there was no burning?
Correction: there was burning.
        burning shame
        burning regret
        burning disappointment (thought i'd got past this)

: shifted to knowing, as the warm pain
spread through my brain
it was met with a fire from the heart
before i had human parents
the universe was my guardian
and it has first rights

        child of the universe
        benevolent, beautiful mystery

knowing
it was not i who
brought the hand down
not i who struck the blows
to the innocent child

remembering
in my gut, those who taught me this
they who first lifted
their hands in violence
against me, an innocent child

i have forgiven myself.
I am still angry at the dead.

Father

I keep thanking God
I have no children.

Your legacy is impeding my progress.
I want my soul and body back.
I want to love and be loved.

Not to be haunted, carrying
your ghost on my weighted shoulder,
facing the world with your grudges.
I have done a daughter's duty.
Now go.

I was always yours.
You owned me before I was out of the womb,
threw Mother around   and around
        heavy with me, a six-month fetus
because she could not spin around you
like a planet on its axis
nor could she forever rise and set upon you
like a moon upon its planet,
but only carry your children to term
if she was lucky.
I tried but could not take her place
sitting, an elfin child, perched
atop the chesterfield
dropping sugar cubes behind for later
waiting with my comb for daddy
to come and sit, and I'd draw it through
the stringy grey hair.

If I remain loyal
        : suffering, as you would
(and all of those around you)

you live on. I have a father.
I might point out that, twenty years ago,
there was no abandonment.
The law parted us.
You were not willing.

Yes, you taught me
how not to cope. And more
than ten years after your prison death
I continue to drag you everywhere.
If I were to change now
it would be to everyone's benefit,
      not to mention
           my own.

Will I concede, then, all of my life
to enter and re-enter
the blood-spattered rooms
of my rage
to recreate the hell and heaven of then?
Is this what we are?
Puppets of the dead?

Don't believe that death is the end,
I tell my lover.
Oh, the dead live on.
It's the so-called living
who exist in backward motions,
swimming for their lost parents
revolving around dead planets

Meanwhile, I swear to God I will not procreate
until after I have truly killed you.
And She understands, and comforts me.
Tells me I'm the ruler of my own universe
and the puller of my own strings.

Stuff It

When the universe
strikes against you again
stuff it down.
seven chocolate bars
a jumbo bag of marshmallows
white and soft and sweeter than sex
stuff them down

wait for nausea to pass
for craving to return:
resume stuffing.

Fill that ugly gaping hole.
resume stuffing (it cannot be called eating)
before craving returns,
before that,
when the nausea becomes slightly muted
you may resume.
the universe struck too hard this time.
a box of chemical-laden,
econo-pak cookies
keeps the day bearable

What you missed,
it's too late now,
even back then he knew
and he filled you with this
to make up for what he could not
give to his own child. (they say he died
from too many chocolate bars.)
so now when it's just too hard
stuff it down.

Stuff
it down.
Stuff it down.
Your body will take over
chewing   swallowing
you can be doing something else
at the same time
you don't even
have to be aware

Stuff it *in*
fill the wound
makes it bigger
but for now, it will do.
Nothing else does it.

You remember puking in the Safeway
he gave us sausage rolls
that were too rich
we sat in the shopping cart
got a fast ride
to the parking lot
two streams of vomit
sweet sisters
we were always sick
together

He stole us away to the island
kept us going on junk food
(there was no use even pretending anymore)
we were put to bed
on a bunk
held to the ceiling by chains

He stood on a chair
holding a sauce pan

in each hand
obediently we leaned over and vomited
filling each of them
neatly to the top
we were all, father and daughters,
polite about it
we all knew
we all understood
this was normal
daddy was the one with the problem
i was seven
but i understood
and i felt sorry for him
and i kept eating
the garbage he gave me

He kept pacing the tiny one-room cabin
when he finally told us
Your mother is dead
it never entered my manipulated mind
to ask, *How?*

Sometimes now
i wish i could puke
thinking back on it
i feel like puking
rejecting his crap
projecting it
across a supermarket
back to the universe
that swallowed him
and mother up

Here, take this
take this back
this is what it's worth

this is how i feel
this is what you fed me
Now you
eat it up

What I've Come From

What I've come from isn't mud.
It isn't the wrong side of the tracks.
What I've come from
is blood and lies.
What I've come from
is human anguish, deep-rooted
and passed down through generations.
It runs in my veins.
But look at me now.
Give me some credit.
My veins are recoiling, spiraling up and out
            and they carry
                            some good blood.

This Phoenix Didn't Rise From Flames

My blood is my own.
My body does not consist
of half his arteries, half hers.
They conceived me
        but I am my own. This
is an entirely fresh
creation.   *See*
the crucial differences.
Faces of my ancestors
in my own face. Their voices
on my lips, memories in the genes
shouting from this throat. This being
is a tapestry of *them and me.*
We're a team.
I live for all of us
in the glory of human evolution
rembering the patterns, sifting them
into the dirt.
Compost.
A whole, new animal.

New Power

She has always felt akin to land
once tampered with, now healed
(patchwork-quilt pastures
framed by old fences)

She walks on an ex-logging road
watching it shrink and soften
under mossy growth

In some places it has become two paths of fine sand
with grass and seedling trees
generously filling in the middle

In others the forest has closed in lovingly
on either side, leaving room
for one meandering, dusty-brown line

Her hands dangle among the fresh tops of plants
legs straddle amiable shrubs

It is June
and her eyes open and close on green

New growth
reaches up to catch sunlight
purify it, turn it lime green

Each fern consists of dark fronds
around the base of earth
with just-unfurled uncurled arms
            pointing up
                        piercing air
with their sharp, clear quality of light
like joyous daggers saluting the sky

Dark, elderly masses of salal
thick, leathery support net
offer up their new babies,
a sea of soft green flames

The sky is chock-full of alder leaves,
whole mandelas of them
dizzying kaleidoscopes

She might believe
there is no other colour

she comes to an arch over the path
naked branches of ancient salal
sunken by time
seeping into her space, the way she must go

she has to squat to get through
sees it all
from a child's point of view

her face crumples
she stands

she has a face now
like something out of a horror flick
this is the only place where she can
do this, wear her grief openly
where all the masks have been stripped
away
and she is a child again, a child
like every innocent new leaf
        torn from its mother bush

she walks in beauty
like a zombie

her mouth is open,
the lips twisted and trembling

the wail is silent (for now)

the nostrils are flared and quivering
the cheeks are white

the forehead is full of lines
frozen
like snakes that writhed in agony
before dying
they make a chaotic map
like too many branches
vying for the sun

the eyes are terrible
they see beauty
take in all of Nature's whispering comforts
here and now
but they cannot be softened
they are wedged in the plane of memory

She imagines another's horror
at seeing her like this.
Some peaceful party taking a stroll
in the woods
minding their own business
catching sight of a bent figure up ahead
out of their own nightmares

they turn and flee in terror
they will not look
at what they themselves
at what we all
have refused to face for so long

She feels the watchfulness
of ferns, salal, alders, birds, sky
        does not mind them seeing.
Knows that this is the place
where she can shed layers of smiles
like a bandage
clean, white, presentable
becoming bloody
as she goes deeper

there is no fear
in showing her true self
to her green friends around her
babies do not turn away

In the forest
she can be a monster-human
        walking slowly, dreadfully
                with new power

Her lips are dry.
She steps up to baby salal
presses the cool, soothing leaf
to her mouth.
Closes her eyes on green.

PART TWO

Seven

I've been seven for two years. I know this, because so
much has happened.

I hardly ever saw my mama, because she was away
reading her poems. She is famous. When school was out we all
went to Mayne Island together. It is my favourite place, and
two whole weeks is a long time of happiness. I did not want it
to end. But mama went away again when we came back home
to the city. We played with Debra down the street, riding our
bikes. Debra has a big, beautiful golden tricycle and her mum
serves Kool-Aid every day to all the kids. Every day she gives us
a different flavour — cherry, raspberry, orange, lemonade. Will
we ever see Debra and her mum again? I don't know.

Me and my sister, we did be quiet and stay out of daddy's
way. In case he got mad and gave us a spanking. We are always
very careful not to spill our milk.

Mama went away for good — to be with another man,
daddy said. When we woke up in the morning, he told us:
"Don't go into the front bedroom this morning, girls." We said,
"okay, daddy." We went to school. The next day he woke us up
in the middle of the night. I know because we had breakfast
when it was dark outside. The lights were on and the windows
were black.

Then we went on the ferry to Mayne Island! Even though
summer was over. We had our two cats with us, Junior and
Tinker, which made the trip extra special. It was fun in the
cabin, except when we were sick. I kept writing my stories. I
drew pictures for my stories. For "The Deer of the Wind" I drew
a stag with large antlers and me in a princess veil. For "The
Adventures of Bobby and His Grandmother" I drew a boy and
an old lady with short curly hair and glasses, like my own Nanna.

I think it was October. We had to go to the new school, and a girl threw a big rock at my eye. It missed, but the blood did drip into my eye. We ran through the fields of waving grass. The teacher washed my forehead with cold water. The girl said, "sorry." She gave me a piggyback. I was on her back when she ran in the game. I felt like a princess, so I forgave her. I still have a scar.

It was raining and there were cows. Daddy told us mama was dead. We both burst out crying. Then I went back to my story. Beth stayed sitting on the chesterfield. She is nine. Daddy walked back and forth inside the room. The next day the men came and took us away from him. We got into the police boat. We were all crying, and daddy was begging them. "Let me say good-bye to my children!"

He stood there as the boat zoomed away. I watched until he was nothing but a dot. The policeman and policewoman on the boat never spoke to us. We were taken to a foster home in Victoria. I liked the backyard. As soon as we walked out the backdoor a steep, green hill sloped down, with arbutus and garry oak trees growing sideways out of it. We would roll down the hill when we felt brave. But I hated the boy there. He chased me all the time. Mostly I read *Charlotte's Web*.

Nanna came and got us from there. We went to her house in North Vancouver. But soon we were in Lynn Valley in another foster home. It was terrible because they were very religious. I got in trouble for having dirty panties and they took away my favourite jean jacket with beads all over it. We had to pray every morning and night. Worst of all, we had to go to Sunday school. There were some fun things, like the whole family had bikes and we all went bike riding together — down a big hill, I nearly lost control. And the dad, he would romp with the kids, us included.

The best time was Easter. Our foster parents hid hundreds of chocolate eggs all over the house. But then Mrs. Boyse told the brother to give some of his eggs to one of his sisters, and he didn't want to. She growled, "Do you want to go to heaven?!" My auntie Brenda was there. I heard her whisper to Nanna. "Let's take these kids out of here."

That night I got in trouble for pouring the rest of my juice back into the container. Then Beth said the supper looked like barf, and she was right. If anyone knows what barf looks like, it's me and my sister. Mrs. Boyse took Beth into the hall and slapped her across the face. After supper the brother told his mum that we were right, all this forced praying and stuff was stupid.

Now we are back at Nanna's. She says religion is a personal thing. I love Nanna but she makes me go to school with my hair in old fashioned ringlets, which I pull out on my way. She makes me wear flood pants sometimes. I change into my gym suit as soon as I get to school, but on the way someone will see me and say something. "Hey Christie pisstie. Floodsaver." I did get an award for creative writing. But I hate school. I hate the kids. They are mean. My older sister Kathy said to take the word Hate out of my vocabulary.

I can't remember my last birthday. I might be eight now but I've told grown-ups what I know. "I've been seven for two years." They never say anything. They just look away.

Jump

NOW STAY THERE, OR YUL BE SORRY.
Bully runs at a twisted side-canter, a malicious crab,
going to get her big sister
and keeping an eye on me (kid caught up in branches)
White face flashes like a patrol car light
as Bully moves down the lane to her house of horrors

it's now or never.
So the child scrambles down
changing definitions as she goes
(Tree: always a sanctuary, now a trap)

hangs by lowest branch
looks at the sharp ground

a few houses down
Bully has reached her backyard.
the moment takes years: hanging child contemplates bare feet
on gravel, fails to decide before
(before)
she sees Bully's mouth making sound
that reaches her like a smack.
HEY! *HEY!*
now shouting for big sister. Nothing for it.
(Jump)

Fear numbs her feet
they carry her feather-light across daggers of rock
now I am one with the children who tread
upon red-hot coals   I feel nothing

Her ankles sprout wings and carry her to her own
backyard, unknown to the sisters.
She won't go in and face parental wrath

WHERE ARE YOUR SHOES?

Alone, her tears feel like hot blood
she rubs her soles on soothing grass.
red and scratched now, stained with streaks of green.
leaves whisper to her.

she hopes for the neighbour's dog
black tail wagging, signal flag of friendship
face beaming, one ear folded and flapping
like a hand waving, harmless.

Interview

1.

I'd had enough of mean girls,
stab-you-in-the-back boys called Rusty
and tough, scary Indian kids who meant business.
I had a chance to start fresh, at twelve years old.
My braces were off, my teeth were free.
I didn't care if it meant travelling
to a school outside my district.
If I went where I was expected
they'd all be there waiting for me.

I even changed my name.
Christie became Christine
and later, Chris. I've never looked back.
In this school nobody knows me
and I'm holding my tongue forever.
But I'm sick of the old woman's rules.
I'm thirteen now — she can't tell me what to do.
John Lennon just died. He'll be my angel
and follow me into this place
they call the group home.

2.

Now I get up every morning at six
to curl my hair, do my makeup
and lie down flat on my back
so's I can do up my zipper.

At the dance I was too cool to do anything
other than let my boyfriend pin me
against the wall.
I was stoned, and wiped out in the hall.
They blamed it on my spike heels.

My boyfriend lost his virginity when he was nine.
It's kind of a thrill, him being so much older
than me — seventeen. He keeps pressuring me
but I won't go all the way.
Not until I'm fifteen. I have principles.

His sister moved into the group home
and I thought she was sixteen.
She's twelve. Lost her virginity at eleven.
I won't be like her.
She gets all the whistles when we go out.

Now I smoke tobacco, pot and sometimes coke.
I swore I'd never do acid, but here I am.
Then Erin, someone even greener than me, moved in.
I begged her to hold out for as long as possible,
but now she's doing it all just like the rest of us.
Lucky it was before her time that Tammy and I
tried ten two-ninety-twos each
developed a wicked rash and were sent to hospital
to throw up.

I have a spiritual connection with John Lennon.
His pictures are all over my wall and I look into his eyes.
I speak to him. He tells me what to do, how to survive.

I had a nice guy once. (The one who's hand
Tammy caught up my skirt as she flew
purposefully into the room, punching on the light.)
But I gave him up for a jerk fresh out of jail
who dumped me when he went to work
at McDonald's. I ran down the dark suburban street
with a knife, threatening to kill myself.
What did Brian do? Walked home.
Now I don't think I can trust anyone.
All I've got is music, the best stuff from the hippie days.

I should have been born then.
One time I tried to overdose on pills, but for once
they had no effect.
Maybe it was John Lennon who saved me.

We broke in to Michelle's parents' house.
Michelle fried some steak. She acted like she owned the place.
In Stanley Park we'd meet her friends,
who got me onto coke and were much older.
They were all men. When one of them started kissing me
I was too shocked to do anything about it.
If she hadn't come into the room at the right time
I wouldn't be a virgin today.
On Davie Street the cops came and we were afraid
they'd think we were hookers.
They took us anyway. I was threatened with a slap
for my mouthy behaviour.

We were always drinking and staggering around
in the bushes at night. I remember the time
Michelle got her period with no pads —
the blood colouring her jeans all the way to her knees!
She betrayed me. They all betrayed me.
Unless I betrayed them first.
One of them screamed at me in the school bathroom:
I hate you and I wish you were dead!
I curse you!
I believe I'm still living under her curse.

And now a girl from my past
has shown up at my highschool.
She wants to kill me.

Tammy ran away with my best friend
two hours ago. They hot-wired a car.
I begged them not to go.

My forty-year-old foster mother is crazy.
She necks with her boyfriend, who gave me
my first hit of acid, in front of us.
She tells us about her sex life.
She declares she is Mary, a "white witch"
and is pregnant with the Second Coming.
We live on white toast and instant noodles.

I try not to listen to her,
but yesterday she made Tammy and I *see* something.
Auras, or ghosts. "Just look at my belly," she coaxed.
"Focus on it ... Now, look around us."
And they were there. Dozens of them.
Gold and silver human outlines of energy,
standing around the table. All different sizes.
Tammy saw them too..
"Mary" didn't stick around; she was out the door and gone
before we could say "Holy shit!"
The visions slowly faded. I was not stoned.

You've heard my side of it.
I can't live there anymore.
My Gram wants me back home, and I'm going.
I've got John in my backpack.
You're the worker. Can you get the place shut down?

46

Scars

For years she went around
with the marks from my nails on her small, pale hands.

Who could have known,
the day that picture was taken
of two babies on two laps
everyone smiling but the newborn;
the yearling reaching over to touch my head
with innocent delight at her new sister
father looking so proud
mother gazing at the child on her knee
        love and devotion
        Who could have known

Long after i learned to smile
the grey faded pictures portray
a sullen, angry toddler.

"Put one foot directly in front of the other.
That way your hips will sway.
Girls should always wiggle their bums
when they walk.
Now who do you love better,
me or your mother?"
"You," i stammered
as she walked into the room
and i looked at her eyes with my shame.

Yet it was she who took the time to teach me
how to ride a two-wheeler without trainers
she who gave me that final push
into freedom and ecstasy
who could have known

i would suddenly feel it skidding and sliding beneath me
    steel rail jamming into my neck.

In the end my sister and i lost them both,
and for a while had only each other.
On the police boat nobody spoke to us
and we, ourselves, were silent.

We were the bane of our mother's family,
barbarous children carrying lice
and impossible behaviours.
No one but the old lady would have us,
and the rest of them tried to talk her out of it.
Who could blame them?
the hair-pulling   *as hard as i could*
the pounding noogies   *lemme at her*
yank a fistful of hair, pummel that skull
get in a few face slaps

She must have got me good, too
— my head always burned afterwards;
but i never felt it in the red of battle.
Too focussed.
Not even sure about the times i scratched her hands
: she must have grabbed me, something i coveted
or uttered a put-down with that skilled tongue
— and out came the nails.
I dug them in. Pulled her skin.
She always told the truth about the marks,
fresh scabs alongside white crescent moons.
"Look what my sister did."
She'd hold out her paws with a smirk
while justice pounded in my chest.

The times hatred and misery were not
squeezing my balloon heart
we weren't serious
and i'd run to my bed or the couch,
flop onto my back and bring my feet up —
an unfailing defense. She would laugh.
And once, at the playground, I stepped on a wasp:
she piggybacked me all the way home.

Some eighteen years later in therapy
I learn we were *normal.*
That it's typical, it's

> *common for troubled children, especially those*
> *who lose their mother or both parents, to take*
> *out their despair viciously on each other.*

"Oh yes," says my therapist, as if it were common knowledge,
"you should see how the Mooge kids are behaving
since Mrs. Mooge died.
There's a war on in their house.
They're like rabid dogs."

I don't know whether to laugh or cry.
Yet now someone takes our picture
and we're both smirking.

The Plan, as Explained by Big Half-Sister

Where did you get these ideas?
You were no burden. We *all* tried to take you kids.
Nobody tried to talk Gramma out of it.
It was your father who put pressure
on Human Resources to place you in foster homes
so he could try for access.
He hadn't been convicted yet;
he still had rights!
Human Resources would arrange
a spying session in a shopping mall.
The family would spot him
sitting somewhere gazing at you
a look of martyrdom on his face
(he fancied himself noble)
and we'd be in uproar: *KEEP HIM
AWAY FROM THESE CHILDREN!*

Don't you remember?

Gramma got sick, so she couldn't keep you —
Human Resources said so.
You were like wild animals:
no one could control you.
Besides being poor, Mum hadn't left him
because she wanted to make it work.
For your sake.
Then he trained you to ignore her instructions.
Only he could control you.

The funeral was risky enough without you,
the media zooming in
as we left the building, all of us
weeping like ferns in the rain.
Next day, the headlines:

MURDERED POET'S FAMILY MOURNS

I looked with dread for the line
but where were the two girls?
and thanked God it wasn't there.

You were too young (and *damaged*) for that kind of chaos.

So much for his "life" sentence:
ten years later the word passed down —
he was to be released on parole.
There was nothing else for it: he would have been
terrorizing us all
for the rest of our lives.
Gramma insisted the contract should be in her name,
since she had the least to lose.
His feet wouldn't have reached the sidewalk.

Librarian

I had enough on my plate, exams
and graduation looming
from the highschool that buoyed me
teachers and friends
who built my self-esteem.
Would he stalk my family
would he come to Gram's house?
Between classes I wrote letters to prison authorities,
sent copies to politicians.
The librarian whose thighs rubbed
her pantyhose together when she waddled
to hush and scold
the librarian whom everyone hated
one day called me into her back room
held my letter out and said "Chris
I found this in the photocopier"
threw her short, thick arms around me
from that point on
was my steadfast friend

inheritance

here it comes, and i can't hold it back
gotta bang my head against this wall, just like he did
try this: smashing forehead into mirror
try this: pounding hands into ears
try this: knuckles on skull
i'm explaining it to you:
i'm plugged in   gotta pull my hair
to disperse the electric hatred
i'd do more if i had the guts
don't you see: this thing that is me is vile
whatever it comes from, dead many years
i'm living, heaving flesh in torment
this is the dr jekyl ms hyde syndrome that is me
never mind about pms. this is me anytime
when we're not looking.
when everything's going alright.
all i gotta do is stand up and start doing something
and she raises her ugly head and ruins all.
i feel her changing the blood cells
to purple, surging into me   sparks flying
gravity spinning   my head into the nearest wall
trying for spontaneous exorcism
only to fall in pieces to the floor, heavy
> *but inside i think i am*
> *petals singed around the edges*
> *floating down the spiral*

as she slowly withdraws like a spent cock
my veins cool off: charred black
satisfied for now, she is grinning maliciously
already planning her next attack

the burning continues for a long time
tears will not put it out

the monster will not accept
    happiness
    a lover's habits
    sunshine and contentment

We must remember it will happen
when we are least expecting her
when things   are going   well

54

instructions

1.
Imagine a person
so dreaded
the news of his death
lifts black weights of tar
from an entire extended family of shoulders
and the whole round, wide sky brightens.
Imagine a man so twisted
the news of his just-in-time expiry
sends people into alternating fits
of cackling laughter
and racked sobs of joy.
Now imagine knowing
he is your source of existence.
This man is your father.

2.
Not anymore. Change *is* to *was*.
He was your father.
It's over.
Get on with your life.

How to Bring Up Children

Stop complaining.
Stop whining.
Read: *you're a worthless little kid and we don't want to hear you.*

Stop crying.
Stop.
               Stop.

all i can see now is the pit.
i live in a beautiful place with a beautiful person
in a country with the highest standard of living in the world.
i don't even complain for the rest of the planet most of the time.

it's more than just whining and crying now.
it's what i call   the Negative Rant.
the list is endless; i begin with a deep breath.
after a while i feel my skin becoming slimy,
my breath turning foul and the fangs growing.
the person i'm criticizing is slumped like a wilted flower
defeated and mute.
My fangs cut into my tongue. Have i won?

my hands are buckled claws with scum under the nails.
my hair is tangled and choked with bitter herbs.

my object raises its head slowly. it speaks, doggedly.
"I'm trying."

And all i want is to save this person from me, then to save me from me
all i want is to be the hummingbird playing territorial tag
flying at warp speed at another (from another)
through the clean air that belongs to none of us.
Disputes among the animals are not only simple
they can be fun.

I want to drop my human form, for good.

I want to be up there with the geese,
so high the clouds kiss the feathers
of their wing tips on the up-stroke.
so far away their voices are faint cries at the back
of our consciousness,
so easy with each other all they have to do is take flight
and the community forms a giant V for efficiency.
I wouldn't even have to be the first one — at the head of the V.
Just one in the long line of friends, encouraging each other
with every honk.
"We're doing great!"   "We're beautiful!"
"Almost there!"

but imagine being the first one!
all of those positive strokes behind you, for miles.
you're the leader of the good-news sky-banner:
the humans below choose to listen and look up in wonder,
stop what they're doing
and watch until you and your clan have passed
over, leaving an impression to be proud of.
a thousand Wingbeats of Now.

August 1, 1991
Mayne Island

And what, dear diary, am I doing on Mayne Island?
Reconnecting to a dear place where I spent childhood summers
until the disaster. Today I sat on a cliff in the rain, staring across
the high tide towards the beloved field where the old wizard,
Gram's brother Bill, lived. When I was working at Value
Village I found (and pounced on) a hardcover edition of his
book, *Science of a Witch's Brew.*

I sat missing him and my mother, and feeling how this
island misses them, still mourns their loss, five and sixteen years
gone respectively. Maybe those two seals I spotted were Uncle
Bill and Auntie Elsie. The heron was Mother, graceful and
cautious.

Last night in Campbell Bay was another spectacular,
almost flourescent sunset. I am falling in love with this planet.
How can I think of doing anything but defending her?
Everything in my life must help me to preserve Earth and her
creatures. It is no chore, it is no drudgery. Mindless jobs are
drudgery. Loving the world is heaven.

I didn't watch the sunset alone — there was a seal and a
shiny otter. I slept outside of the tent, under the stars, and was
rewarded by five bright shooting stars with long tails.

Yesterday I went wandering, barefoot. I wanted to hug
the rocky, mossy land, crunch-step in the leaves, climb the
arbutus trees — but I just cried and cried. Every time I thought
I was finished and started to head back to the tent, I'd start
again. I was mourning for the dead, for those left alive, for my
childhood, and for finally being in places I've long dreamed of
revisiting. I'm actually here on Mayne. This is not a dream.

Everyone here is doing well, the world keeps a-turning — for
those left to turn with it. I've learned that death is a real,
essential part of life, and that sorrow is the same of joy.

Near our tent lies a decayed remnant of a chipmunk. Its
tiny paw waves in the wind. And when I was walking along in
tears, a chipmunk scrambled up a branch over my head,
scolding, very much alive.

True Love

All power and deepest love to she who cries.
The survivor is thriver. Strength to her!
She is here for the long haul.
We call on the goddess Kali —
give us the ability to transform!
Hear our prayer and invocation ...
      I am never alone!
      I feel love showering all around me,
      entering all my pores.
      I am all noticed;
      I am all attended to.
      I am appreciated.
      My cup overflows with love.
      My tears are hot with it. It tingles
      to the ends of my hair
      — shimmering sparks of love.
      I float on the nectar of the sweet Goddess
      my mother, who loves me deeply and forever.
      Her love drips off the ends of my fingers
      and from the lobes of my ears.
      I am bejewelled with our divine affection.
      I sleep under the blanket of adoration.
      I am wrapped in the cocoon of esteem.
      The green grass of admiration grows
      thick as weeds around me.
      Notice and attention are showered upon
      my peaceful, sleeping self,
      as a million precious rose petals.
      I roll, dream, and wake in a fountain of love.
      I rise and walk through lifegiving air,
      I wash in healing balm,
      I dress beside a welcoming heart of fire,
      and the mighty earth proudly holds me up.

Changing

I watch you from above, I am sitting on a branch in a tree.
I follow behind, running on the trail after you.
I watch you hurting yourself.
I hear you weep.
I wait for you now, ahead on the trail.
You stagger up to me, sobbing.
You stop and gasp at the sight of me.
I am weeping with love and compassion.
I understand your pain.
I open my arms.
You rush in.
I hold you. In our embrace is healing.
We fit perfectly, being exactly the same height and shape.
Our hair is the same, and tickles our wet faces,
sticks to them.
I look into your face.
Such deep, wrenching sorrow in your eyes.
Slowly it is changing to relief and hope,
the look of someone who is loved.
Your cheeks are red from the slaps, your head aches.
You won't go down to the dock.
You don't need to go through this anymore.
I have found you.
I will hug you forever.
You disappear, I am hugging myself.
Keep me in your heart.

July 15, 1994

There was fog at Tonquin beach yesterday morning, white as snow. Between billowing clouds of it I saw black birds swooping, and I could hear their calls. Crows were dive-bombing a raven. I called out: my best raven-croak. The raven seemed to answer.

Last night I dreamt it was my mother, her hair turned to feathers, her hands turned to wings. She perched upon a tall stump beside the trail. She was making a myriad of raven sounds, all in an effort to communicate with me. I could not, however I tried, understand her language, and I awoke in tears.

What were you trying to tell me?

What's Left For Me

1.

I toss it lightly
from hand to hand
a small cardboard box
with the words:
Cremated Remains of.
October 1975.
Inside, an empty plastic bag.
At the bottom,
a crumb of ash
no more significant than a few
grains of sand.
All substantial evidence,
thick grey matter i could have
held in my hand,
rubbed between my fingers,
clumps of solid bone
i could have cupped and caressed
in my palms,
gone.

2.

Is it possible to bathe
in a crumb of ash?
The act would erase it
and truly, then, I'd have nothing.
But oh, to roll it around
in my closed fist like dice

to smell it, fearful of sniffing too hard
and losing it
like an addict hurriedly inhaling
one last pinprick of cocaine.

I can just see myself:
endless self-inflicted sneezing

to rub it over my hands like lotion
watching it grow smaller and smaller
like the incredible shrinking woman
you were.
To smear it onto my face
and the tears wash it away forever.
To finally decide, *I've got it:*
she'll be a part of me always.
      Eat the ash.
Next day only to end up crazy,
frantically searching my stool.

No, what's left shall remain
in its cardboard box, safely
put away in my sister's closet.
I'll not even steal it and encase it
in a pendant to be lost
down the meaningless well
of single earrings and socks.
The only vortex you'll be sucked into
is the big one:
our collective hearts.

Postscript

Still Reaching

Reaching for you was like struggling toward an island against the tide. Reaching you is like reaching the shore, held out like a hand.

I've been reaching for you since childhood, all through my teenage years — nothing but imposters. But I was reaching for survival, the water that would save me for I was wilting and parched ...

I did not reach to give but to take.

My hands finally touched you: I was saved.

Time to give. You've been giving for seven years. I take that and ego-swell with pride — always reaching for years together, safe, committed; "I've done it." *We've* done it. Seven, the magic number. I can say I've finally, truly reached you. You keep holding onto me so I won't fall and I check to make sure you're holding onto yourself, too. Thanks to both of us I share in the holding, trying to make an adult out of a thirty-year-old child (who's scared, thinks it's the past). The adult reaches for herself ... I reach for my self ... for the now, the moment, you/ love (the same wonder)

and

make new, fresh, unheard of,
creative choices.

The Visit

Only we can recognize your face. The original version has been disguised, almost hidden, by age.

I visit you where you live. I know it's a home for the elderly. You insist on calling it a hospital. Hospitals are temporary. Patients go home eventually. Well, this too is temporary. One day you will go Home.

Today you tell me of how you paid $45 for a perm that didn't take. How it's $16 every time you just want to get it set. And how the stylist keeps pestering you to come back for another try.

I wheel you to the sink so you can wet your comb. "I don't like my ears showing," you tell me. You point to a brush; "This is mine, and someone else has been using it." I wonder how you know. It is filled with white hair. There aren't too many variations around here.

Amid the blotches and lines I recognize you, Virginia: mother of my mother.

*   *   *

I wheel you to a table where yours is one of the names taped to the surface. You introduce me to a friend or two. "This is Lottie. Lottie, this is my grandaughter from the island."

You tell me the old cherry tree is diseased and will soon be cut down. I always knew, so why the shock?

"Yes, I loved it too. I used to stand on the verandah and bask in the white mass of loveliness."

You used to ask me to come down, worried I was
climbing too high. But tree climbing was my one area of
confidence and I stayed put, reassuring you from my perch.

You were just doing your job.

I sat in the highest throne of branches, reading my
Narnia books. When I finished the last in the series I'd often
start again at the beginning. I'd carry the book in my teeth so
my arms were free to grasp and swing me far away from the
ground. I still have the originals, each with teeth marks on the
upper right corner.

In spring I worshipped the blossoms. Near school's end I
feasted on cherries from Heaven. Other kids would come
walking by and make fun of me, climbing trees at my age. A
stoned teenager, I sat in the tree adding too many cherries to
the hash in my stomach. I held the fat, dark, juice-laden fruit up
to the sun. Reverence. I became one with the cherries. Then
retreated, doubled over, to bed.

*   *   *

You tell me you don't know the name of the disease. You
say they will replace the tree, plant a new one. The others were
not replaced; why should the merciless change their habits now?
I know I would recognize it, even dismembered, taken from us,
disappearing down the street in the back of some pickup truck.
But you are speaking, giving advice.

"When you settle on your bit of land, don't get an early
cherry: there aren't enough bees, and what with the wind and
rain the blossoms can't get established."

Oh, they got established alright. The yearly mass of
white loveliness. It is old age that has ravaged our cherry tree. It

cannot be replaced. Why, it would be like trying to replace the years.

First they chopped down the crab apple, next the dogwood, now the cherry. The dogs both died within weeks of each other — years of costly grooming didn't help. We'll all meet again, the trees, the dogs, you and the rest of us, one day when we all get home. Until then, we remember. We recognize.

Until our next visit, I retreat to my island.

Last

The spot on the couch where i'd sit by the stove.
The blanket too.
My books, well-loved, some read and re-read, others neglected.
My pens, crayons, felts, gluestick, colouring book;
my fifteen scrapbooks and albums full of pictures.
My side of the bed.
A well-worn pair of sandals that won't fit you.
A crazy collection of clothes to bewilder you.
My system of where things belong.
My marbles, shells and beadwork.
My painted hats, hanging on their nails.
The memory of my fist shattering the window,
the meteor showers of hot tears,
peace after the drama.
And all my words. Stacks of journals
filling dusty, worn suitcases — all yours.
Forgive me now,
before you start reading.

72

A Selection of Our Titles in Print

96 Tears (in my jeans) (R.M. Vaughan)	0-921411-65-0	3.95
Best Lack All, The (Tom Schmidt)	0-921411-37-5	12.95
CHSR Poetry Slam: Speaking Poetry (Andrew Titus, editor)	1-896647-06-5	9.95
Coils of the Yamuna (John Weier)	0-921411-59-6	14.95
Cover Makes a Set (Joe Blades)	0-919957-60-9	8.95
Cranmer (Robert Hawkes)	0-921411-66-9	4.95
Crossroads Cant (Mary Elizabeth Grace, Mark Seabrook, Shafiq, Ann Shin, Joe Blades (ed.))	0-921411-48-0	13.95
Dark Seasons (Georg Trakl; Robin Skelton (trans.))	0-921411-22-7	10.95
for a cappuccino on Bloor (kath macLean)	0-921411-74-X	13.95
Gift of Screws (Robin Hannah)	0-921411-56-1	12.95
Heaven of Small Moments (Allan Cooper)	0-921411-79-0	12.95
Herbarium of Souls (Vladimir Tasic)	0-921411-72-3	14.95
I Hope It Don't Rain Tonight (Phillip Igloliorti)	0-921411-57-X	11.95
In the Dark: Poets & Publishing (Joe Blades)	0-921411-62-6	9.95
Invisible Accordion, An (Jennifer Footman, editor)	0-921411-38-3	14.95
Like Minds (Shannon Friesen)	0-921411-81-2	14.95
Lad from Brantford, A (David Adams Richards)	0-921411-25-1	11.95
Longing At Least Is Constant (Kathryn Payne)	0-921411-68-5	12.95
New Power (Christine Lowther)	0-921411-94-4	11.95
Notes on drowning (rob mclennan)	0-921411-75-8	13.95
Open 24 Hours (Anne Burke; D.C. Reid; Brenda Niskala; Joe Blades, rob mclennan)	0-921411-64-2	13.95
Poems for Little Cataraqui (Eric Folsom)	0-921411-28-6	10.95
Manitoba highway map (rob mclennan)	0-921411-89-8	13.95
Memories of Sandy Point (Phyllis Pieroway)	0-921411-33-2	14.95
Milton Acorn Reading from More Poems for People. (Milton Acorn)	0-921411-63-4	9.95
Railway Station (karl wendt)	0-921411-82-0	11.95
Rant (Sabrina Fowler-Ferguson)	0-921411-58-8	4.95
Rum River (Raymond Fraser)	0-921411-61-8	16.95
Seeing the World with One Eye (Edward Gates)	0-921411-69-3	12.95
Song of the Vulgar Starling (Eric Miller)	0-921411-93-6	14.95
Speak! (Jim Larwill; et al)	0-921411-45-6	13.95
St Valentine's Day (Jennifer Footman)	0-921411-45-6	13.95
Strong Winds (Sheila Hyland, editor)	0-921411-60-X	14.95
Túnel de proa verde / Tunnel of the Green Prow (Nela Rio; Hugh Hazelton, translator)	0-921411-80-4	13.95
Under the Watchful Eye (James Deahl)	0-921411-30-8	11.95

www.brokenjaw.com coming soon for secure e-Commerce online ordering. Direct from the publisher, all individual orders must be prepaid. Canadian orders must add 7% GST/HST (Revenue Canada Business Number 12489 7943 RT0001).

Sales representation: **Literary Press Group of Canada**, ph 416 483-1321, www.lpg.ca
Trade order fulfilment: **General Distribution Services**, 325 Humber College Blvd, Toronto ON M9W 7C3, Canada: Telephone: Toronto, 416 213-1919 ext 199, Ont/Que 1-800-387-0141; Atlantic, Western Canada, NW Ontario 1-800-387-0172, fax 416 213-1917;Telebook (CTA) S 1150391, customer.service@ccmailgw.genpub.com ; USA 1-800-805-1083, gdsinc@genpub.com , Pubnet 6307949.

BROKEN JAW PRESS
BOX 596 STN A
FREDERICTON NB E3B 5A6
CANADA

tel / fax: 506 454-5127
www.brokenjaw.com